LET'S WALK THERE!

Series Editor: Bruce Bedford

Northern Scotland

Cameron McNeish

Line drawings by Dudley Evans

JAVELIN BOOKS

POOLE · NEW YORK · SYDNEY

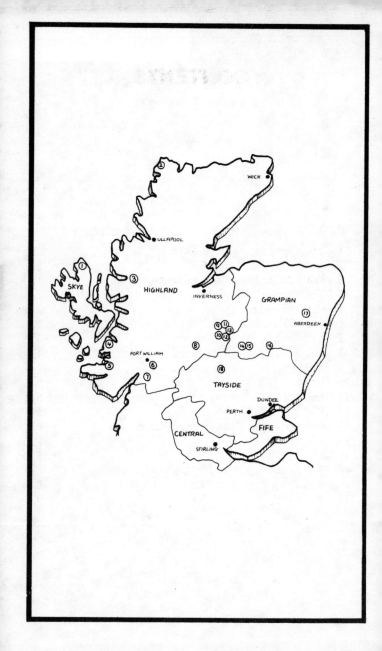

CONTENTS

First published in the UK 1987 by Javelin Books,
Link House, West Street, Poole, Dorset, BH15 1LL

Copyright © 1987 Javelin Books

Distributed in Australia by
Capricorn Link (Australia) Pty Ltd,
PO Box 665, Lane Cove, NSW 2066

British Library Cataloguing in Publication Data

McNeish, Cameron
    Northern Scotland. — (Let's walk there!)
    1. Walking —Scotland —Guide-books
    2. Scotland —Description and travel —
    1981- —Guide-books
    I. Title II. Series
    914.11'103858   DA870

Cover picture:
Eileen Donan Castle courtesy of The British Tourist
Authority, Britain on View (BTA/ETB)

Cartography by Ron Rigby

Typeset by Inforum Ltd, Portsmouth
Printed in Great Britain by Cox & Wyman Ltd, Reading, Berks

INTRODUCTION

As worthwhile as any walk might be, it becomes doubly appealing if it takes you to some place of special interest. The nine books in this series, covering England, Scotland and Wales were conceived to describe just such walks.

A full description of the walk's objective is given at the start of each chapter. The objectives are diverse, giving a wide choice. Most are non-seasonal, and involve little walking in themselves once you are there.

Following the description of the objective, each section of the walk is clearly described, and a specially drawn map makes route-finding straightforward. As well as detailing the route, the authors describe many subsidiary points of interest encountered along the way.

The walks are varied and easy to follow. None of them is too taxing, except in the severest weather. Most are circular, returning you to your car at the starting point. Family walkers with young children will find plenty of shorter routes to suit their particular needs, whilst those with longer legs can select from more substantial walks.

The routes have been carefully chosen to include only well-established routes, and readers will certainly increase the enjoyment which they and others derive from the countryside if they respect it by following the Country Code.

Bruce Bedford
Series Editor

Walk 1
THE QUIRAING, ISLE OF SKYE
HIGHLAND
2 miles

Skye has never had a great reputation amongst walkers, possibly because of its reputation as a Mecca for rock climbers and scramblers. Without any shadow of doubt the rocky spires and pinnacles of the Black Cuillin offer some of the finest mountaineering terrain in the country, but it would be a terrible injustice to ignore the Isle of Skye from the walker's point of view.

The Trotternish Peninsula that stretches northwards from the island's capital town, Portree, offers some fine walking terrain. For almost the full length of the peninsula runs the great feature of Trotternish, a long winding escarpment of basalt cliffs, running in a southerly direction from the steep peaks of Sgurr Mhor and Sron Vourlinn near Duntulm to the bare moorland above Portree.

The sheer east-facing cliffs of this great ridge are sills, or sheets of lava, immensely thick, intruded between the upper and lower layers of the basalt plateaux, after they were laid down. The upper basalt sheets have been cut back to the ridge, and have left the long intrusive sills in a long line from Portree, up the length of the peninsula, and out to sea as far north as the Shiant Isles.

While the east-facing cliffs are sheer, the western slopes of the ridge are in complete contrast. Long gentle grassy slopes run all the way to the rim of the cliffs, the turf shorn short and smooth by the continual grazing of sheep and rabbits and by the constant caress and occasional batterings of the westerly breezes.

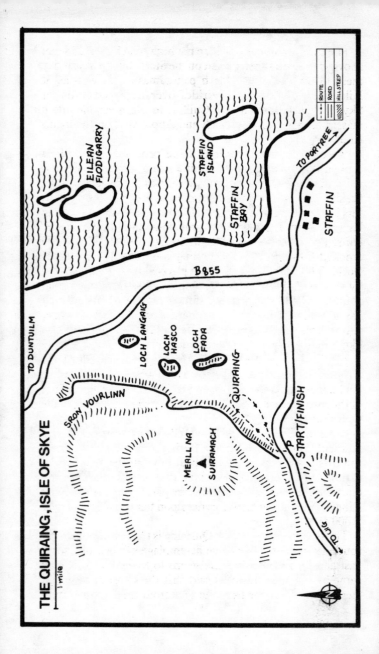

THE QUIRAING, ISLE OF SKYE

1 mile

EILEAN FLODIGARRY

STAFFIN ISLAND

STAFFIN BAY

TO PORTREE

STAFFIN

B855

TO DUNTULM

LOCH LANGAIG

LOCH HASCO

LOCH FADA

QUIRAING

SRON VOURLINN

MEALL NA SUIRAMACH

P

START/FINISH

TO UIG

ROUTE
ROAD
HILL STEEP

The summits of the ridge are not high, reaching 2,358 feet above sea level at the trig point on the Storr, but on a clear day these lowly hills offer superb panoramas as far west as St Kilda, beyond the Outer Hebrides, over the jagged outline of Skye's chief attraction, the Cuillin, to the great mountain masses of Torridon, Gareloch and Applecross on the mainland.

Close to the northern end of the peninsula, the cliff is broken up into a strange amphitheatre of spires, rocks and volcanic debris which has split away from the rock face of the basalt cliffs. Sited below the summit of Meall na Suiramach, this is the Quiraing, meaning a fold or pen. Only in volcanic Iceland have I ever seen formations like those in the Quiraing; contorted, bent, and strangely malevolent, like crooked fingers of rock beckoning you towards some other world. The mystic quality of the place is further emphasized by the lavish lushness of the slopes. Wild flowers grow in abundance, and the grass is an intense shade of green which has a tendency to soften the harshness of the landscape, almost creating a surrealistic effect. There is nowhere else like it in Scotland. It is unique and more than worth a visit.

Just south of the Quiraing, the long escarpment of the Trotternish ridge is breached by a road which runs across the backbone of the peninsula from Staffin to Uig. At the summit of the road there is a car park and this is where the track to the Quiraing begins.

Cross the road to the track and follow it eastwards as it rises gradually across the hillside, offering some fine views down towards Staffin and over the peat bogs to the sea and the mainland of Scotland. This track is a remarkably beautiful one with the wide sweep of the shore paralleling the sweeping fringe of the ridge which rises tier upon tier to a height of over 2,000 feet.

The first indication of the Quiraing is the Prison, the folds' southerly outpost, a massive assemblage of rock like some vast ancient fortress. No-one seems to know how this rock came by its name, but it is said that the ghost of some old cleric used to emerge from the rock from time to time, until

The Quiraing, a volcanic landscape freak of nature.

eventually he was put to rest by some good and kindly person.

Long dark corridors now take you away from the open slope and up past the towering spire of the Needle, 120 feet in height and tapering both at the top and the bottom. Above you immense crags, blocks and screes loom high, the slope leading upwards into the giant amphitheatre. Great slices of rock, fissured, weathered and cracked, stand apart from the main cliff behind, and through these great fissures you can gaze out to the contrasting pastoral scene below – the tiny crofts shrunk into insignificance, the green fields rolling and soft, and the swell of the sea breaking its surf on the great curve of Staffin Bay.

But another surprise awaits you. In this world of Titan verticalities, of grey and black upthrusts, it seems almost unreal to come across a high rounded table of lush cropped grass, as flat and smooth as a bowling green. This is the Table, the jewel of the Quiraing. A slanting ledge runs onto the surface of this wide upthrust, and behind it, perhaps in sympathy with the lushness of the unexpected turf, the riven

10

cliff face is a veritable rock garden. Yellow globe flowers, red and white campions, blue butterwort and sprays of golden roseroot offer a splash of colour to the shining black rock; the Hanging Gardens of Babylon couldn't have been finer. This could well have been the setting for Tolkien's Rivendell, home of Elrond and his Elvin folk, a magical place on a magical island.

You can return to the road by either the same path as you came up, or else drop down one of the steepish scree corridors eastwards, where another track circumnavigates the Quiraing. Once clear of the cliffs the path can be followed southwards then westwards and back to the Staffin-Uig road.

Walk 2
SANDWOOD BAY
HIGHLAND
4½ miles

If you're one of those people who can sit for hours entranced by the continuous motion of pounding waves, then Sandwood Bay is a marvellous place to visit. Of course, those ancient Celts who lived by the sea had their lives dominated by the pulse of the tides, and many now believe that the moon, the co-ordinator of the tides, held a special significance for these sea-going people.

One finds it easy to comprehend all this in Sandwood Bay as great Atlantic rollers surge continuously into two miles of gently curving bay fringed by whiter than white sands, sands that are in turn fringed by these impetuous tides breaking eagerly from pale green swell into white foam. Bisecting the sands runs a long line of marram grass dunes; behind lies a vast acreage of white sand, like some far-flung desert.

Away at the southern end of the bay a solitary sea-stack rises from the water to guard the place. Called Am Buachaille, or the Shepherd, it is a tall tower of Torridonian sandstone which is a skyscraper of fulmar petrels.

Behind the bay the large freshwater Sandwood Loch holds back the bleakness of the Sutherland moors, and gives the whole place a depth of feeling that is lacking in most coastal areas. To the north green headlands roll down to the sea before tumbling into the Atlantic in precipitous cliffs, and beyond the farthest of them the white tower of the Cape Wrath lighthouse, the most north-westerly point of the British mainland, lifts its head above the curving land.

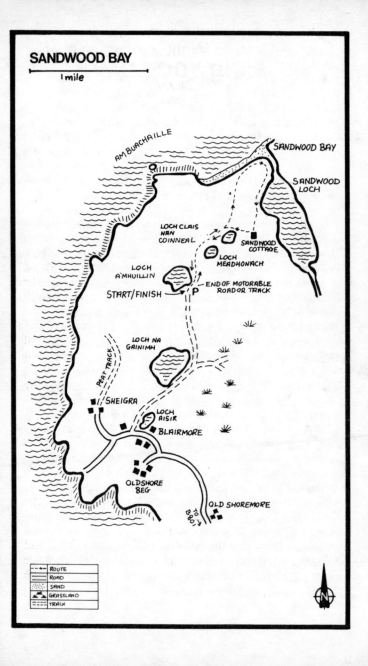

Sandwood Bay is singularly aloof and very lonely. Atmospherically the place is splendid and it's perhaps little wonder that this, of all the bays on the western seaboard, is supposed to be the hauling-up place for mermaids. Sandy Gunn, a shepherd, was walking in the marram grass sand dunes when his dog came running to him in some distress. Inquisitive, Sandy approached the spot where his dog had come from, a long spur of rock running out to sea near the southern end of the bay. There, at the seaward end of the spur, was a mermaid, sunning herself on a ledge. When the mermaid looked up and appeared to gaze in his direction, Sandy, now terrified, withdrew.

Trapped between the crashing breakers of the Atlantic and the rolling wilderness of the Sutherland moors, Sandwood Bay seems to infiltrate the spirit with a feeling of intense isolation – a feeling that to some people can be almost overpowering. There is, I am convinced, a fusion of one's own spirit and the very essence of that isolation, so that when you leave the place it's as though you are leaving a part of your soul there behind you.

Sandwood Bay is reached from the tiny hamlet of Oldshore Beg, some three miles north-west of Kinlochbervie in Sutherland. A peat road leaves the motor road between Blairmore and Sheigra, and a sign on the gate indicates that you can drive your car as far as Loch a'Mhuillin, saving, if you like, two miles walk in either direction. The peat road runs flat past the lochs of Loch Aisir and Loch na Gainimh, to Loch a'Mhuillin, where there is a good turning area. The rest of the route to the bay follows a good track across the rolling moors.

The walk across these moors isn't terribly exciting, but go on an early summer's evening and you will be accompanied by the 'drumming' of snipe and the 'birling' of golden plover, both birds of the wide open moors. Follow the track for two miles past Loch Meadhonach and Loch Clais nan Coinneal. Just after this second loch the path splits in two, the left-hand route taking you downhill into the bay, and the other leading to the ruin of Sandwood Cottage.

Mermaids and ghosts frequent Sandwood Bay amid the crashing Atlantic and the sound of gulls.

Follow the track down to the bay and enjoy the atmosphere of it in the company of fulmar petrels, kittiwakes, razorbills, seals and – if you're lucky, as I was – otters.

Return to your car by crossing the great area of sand immediately behind the marram grass dunes and skirt the northern edges of Sandwood Loch. On the hill above the loch you'll see the red roofed Sandwood Cottage, used nowadays as a walkers' shelter. This is well worth a visit because there is a strange story attached to it. It relates to an Edinburgh woman who was given, as a souvenir of the remotest dwelling in Scotland, a fragment of wood from the broken staircase in the house.

Since the fragment came into her possession, strange things have occurred in her house. Crockery has tumbled to the floor for no apparent reason, knocks and heavy footsteps have been heard from time to time, and on one occasion she caught the smell of strong drink and tobacco before glimpsing the outline of a bearded sailor. She has never visited Sandwood Bay or Sandwood Cottage, and she did not know that the bay, and particularly the cottage, is said to be haunted by the ghost of a bearded sailor who has been seen from time to time by fishermen, shepherds and sailors. An intriguing tale.

An alternative return route to Oldshore Beg is possible by following the cliff tops back from Sandwood Bay. This adds considerably to the distance and the going is very rough with a lot of up and down, but may appeal to stronger and more experienced walkers.

Walk 3
COIRE MHIC FHEARCHAIR OF BEINN EIGHE
HIGHLAND
5 miles

No walking guide to the northern parts of Britain would be complete without at least a reference to Torridon, one of the most scenic parts of this country. I've chosen a walk to what I think is possibly the grandest of all Scottish mountain corries, Coire Mhic Fhearchair. It's a there-and-back rather than circular walk, but the scenery is so impressive I'm sure you won't mind seeing it twice.

If you go to Coire Mhic Fhearchair in the autumn then the surrounding moors and the corrie itself resound to the sound of rutting stags. Don't be fooled into thinking the white summits of these great hills are snow-capped – the quartzite tops of the Torridon mountains tend to be light grey in colour, similar to snow. But by late autumn it could well be snowing on the high tops, and in the depths of winter Coire Mhic Fhearchair is a grand sight indeed with its ice-encrusted buttresses, scalloped cornices above, and the lochan hidden under a mantle of white.

In 1967 the National Trust for Scotland took into its care on behalf of the nation the 14,000 acre estate of Torridon which includes some of the finest mountains in Scotland. The Trust's property includes Liathach and Beinn Alligin, the southern slopes of Beinn Dearg to its skyline, and the southern slopes of Beinn Eighe from the summit ridge of Sail Mhor to Spidean Coire nan Clach. The two principal mountains in the group, Liathach and Beinn Eighe, are outstanding for the grandeur of their corries, crags, pinnacles and

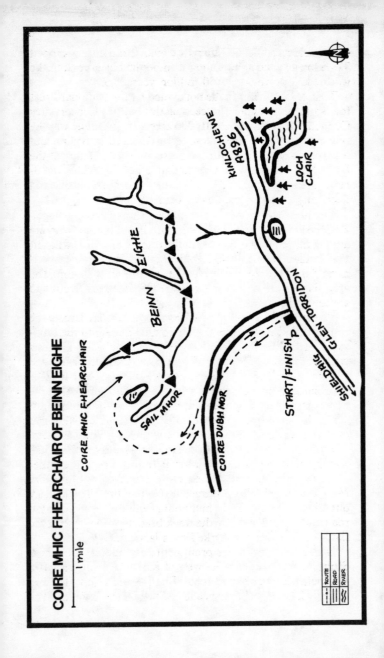

COIRE MHIC FHEARCHAIR OF BEINN EIGHE

1 mile

COIRE MHIC FHEARCHAIR

BEINN

EIGHE

SAIL MHOR

COIRE DUBH MOR

START/FINISH P

GLEN TORRIDON

SHIELDAIG

KINLOCHEWE A896

LOCH CLAIR

| ROUTE |
| ROAD |
| RIVER |

soaring ridges. The mountains are made from quartz-capped Torridonian sandstone, thought to be the oldest rock in the world, laid down some 750 million years ago.

That part of Beinn Eighe not owned by the National Trust for Scotland is under the care of the Nature Conservancy Council. This covers over 10,000 acres. Beinn Eighe was the first National Nature Reserve to be declared in Britain and was acquired primarily for the preservation and study of the fairly large remnant of Caledonian pinewood. The woodlands are being extended within enclosed areas so that red deer can't graze on the newly formed shoots.

The mountain slopes of Beinn Eighe are of great geological, physiographical and floristic interest. Pine martens are among the animals protected in the reserve as well as wildcat, fox, badger, buzzard and golden eagle. Research work is carried out here from the nearby Anancaun field station. The area displays all the main rocks and there are many Arctic and alpine plants.

The steep-sided valleys and prominent hills are largely the result of glaciation when the ice gouged deep into the sandstone. The result has been superb montane relics like this walk's objective, Coire Mhic Fhearchair, great deeply eroded and ice smoothed hollows. Coire Mhic Fhearchair itself is dominated by a great triple buttress of light grey quartzite which stands on an equally impressive plinth of red sandstone, looming over a rock cradled lochan which spills out over the corrie lip into a series of white falls and cascades.

From the outflow of the lochan a track curves west then south round the base of Sail Mhor to link up with another track in Coire Dubh. The shortest walking route to Coire Mhic Fhearchair is by this track up Coire Dubh. The journey out takes about two and a half hours from the Glen Torridon road and the point where the track branches uphill along the flank of Sail Mhor is marked by a large cairn.

Leave your car in the prominent roadside car park near Slugach, about seven miles west of Kinlochewe on the A896 Kinlochewe to Torridon road. The path is signposted and initially follows the stream called Allt Coire an Anmoich. The

Coire Mhic Fhearchair of Beinn Eighe, one of the most exciting corries in the Scottish highlands.

path is a good one and rises gently into the narrow confines of Coire Dubh Mor, the Big Dark Corrie. This is a superb situation, with the great flank of Beinn Eighe on your right, and the castellated buttresses of Liathach on your left – two of the finest mountains in the country.

As you begin to descend from the summit of the pass you'll come across a small lochan beside the track. Just opposite this you'll find the cairn I referred to earlier, so take the right-hand branch of the track and follow it gently uphill in a north-easterly direction around the flanks of Sail Mhor. Below you lie the waters of Loch nan Cabar, and if you stop and look behind you, and the weather is clear, you'll enjoy a tremendous view of the rugged cliffs, buttresses and corries of the north flanks of Liathach, truly a remarkable sight.

The path continues to rise gently and then rather steeply before the grandeur of the Coire Mhic Fhearchair bursts into view.

As you wander round this path, and as you return to Glen Torridon, keep your eyes peeled for some of the fauna of

Torridon. Although not numerous, this offers a fine variety, from the red deer, Britain's largest mammal, to the pygmy shrew, its smallest. If you are really lucky you might hear the call of greenshank from one of the hill lochans, or the eerie call of the great northern diver. In September and October these glens reverberate to the sound of the stag rut. Take some binoculars and try and spot one of the stags as it lifts its head back and roars like a great lion. The sound of it is the very epitome of the highland wilderness, a primeval roar. Buzzards may wheel above the roadside, but as you wander up the length of Coire Dubh Mor you're more likely to see an even greater bird of prey, the golden eagle. The golden plover may well entertain you with its melancholy whistle, and higher up towards the Coire Mhic Fhearchair itself you'll possibly hear the gruntings and cackle of grouse and even ptarmigan, the bird of the high tops.

Walk 4
THE VIEW TO THE ISLES
HIGHLAND
8 miles

This fine circular walk, which starts and finishes in the fishing village and ferry port of Mallaig, gives you a superb view out across the harbour towards the outer isles. Mallaig is very much the culmination point of the traditional Road to the Isles. It's here the road ends, and if you want to go further, then it has to be by boat.

It's worthwhile taking this short walk, for the view is unparalleled. The vast seaward panorama encompasses the mountain ranges from south and north, from the distant Point of Ardnamurchan, the most westerly point on the British mainland, to the great horseshoe of the Cuillin hills of Skye, then beyond to the Sound of Sleat and Kintail. In between lie the Small Isles, Rhum of the craggy Cuillin-like mountains, and Eigg and Canna, remarkably flat compared with the mountains that lie all around you.

Especially close to you are the great mountains of Knoydart, that vast wilderness area that lies in a peninsula bounded by Loch Hourn, the Loch of Hell, and Loch Nevis, the Loch of Heaven. Trapped in its mountain limbo, between heaven and hell, Knoydart is a magnificent area that is both roadless and, for the most part, unpopulated.

If the weather is clear, you may well see beyond the Small Isles to the Outer Hebrides – the rocky hills of Harris and the long flat expanse of Lewis – and maybe, if you are exceptionally lucky, even beyond that to lonely St Kilda on the edge of the Atlantic.

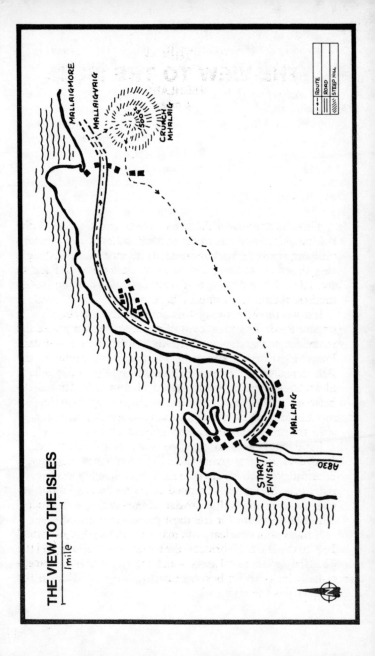

THE VIEW TO THE ISLES

1 mile

MALLAIGMORE

MALLAIGVAIG

CRUACH
MHALAIG

500

MALLAIG

START
FINISH

A830

ROUTE
ROAD
STEEP HILL

N

Mallaig lies at the end of the West Highland Railway, the railway journey from Fort William that is claimed to be one of the finest in the country. Yet even better than this sixty mile journey is the train ride from Glasgow. You can sit back and enjoy the scenic delights of Loch Lomondside, the beauty of Strathfillan, and the wide open expanses of the bare Rannoch Moor before the train follows the line of Loch Trieg towards the gorge at Tulloch and the long miles of Glen Spean. Have lunch in Fort William, the capital of the western highlands, and rejoin the train again for its afternoon run along the banks of Loch Eil, to Glenfinnan at the head of Loch Shiel, past Loch an Uamh where Bonnie Prince Charlie left Scotland after his ill-fated attempt at uprising, and on towards the white sands of Arisaig and Morar.

The train stops at Mallaig, and here many people continue their journey out towards the Hebrides, to the Isle of Skye or Rhum, to Eigg and Canna. There are motor-boat cruises, too, to Loch nan Uamh and Loch Moidart, to Loch Scavaig in Skye, to Loch Duich in Kintail and to Loch Hourn in Knoydart. Indeed, if that great wilderness area of Knoydart is your destination, then it's from Mallaig you will sail, across the wide expanse of Loch Nevis to Inverie.

Mallaig is a magical sort of a place. Always busy, it is noisy with the cacophony of gulls, eager to catch a small piece of fish from one of the fishing boats. The harbour is very much the centre of activity. Mallaig is a specialised fishing port, and after fishing all else seems to be ignored. The harbour is the focal point for visitors, too, enjoying the sights and sounds of the fleet, the bustle of landing the catch and despatching it on its way to the south. Fifty herring boats use the harbour, and the lobster fleet fishes two thousand miles of coastline, making Mallaig the most important herring and shellfish port of the west coast. You'll hear the broad brogue of north-east Scotland mix with the gentle softness of the West Highland accents, for each Monday morning the fishing fleet crews arrive from their homes in Aberdeenshire and Banffshire, travelling these great distances to fish the best waters in the country.

The end of the Road to the Isles: the view to the Inner Hebrides and beyond.

The walk starts on the east side of the harbour bay, along a public road which runs for a mile or so above the bay and through a small housing estate. Once clear of the houses the road runs alongside the hillside to the tiny crofting community of Mallaigvaig. Down below you lie the waters of the outer Loch Nevis, and across its silvery expanse the hills of Knoydart lie serene. It was here that Bonnie Prince Charlie landed on his escape from Skye on July 5th, 1746, during his post-Cullodon flight from the troops of the government and the Duke of Cumberland.

Beyond Mallaigvaig a track, known locally as the Burma Road, continues for three-quarters of a mile to the croft at Mallaigmore. Half-way along this track, climb the slopes to the fine vantage point of Cruach Mhalaig, where you will be amply rewarded for your efforts by the superb views across to the Small Isles. However, if you don't feel inclined to climb the hill to Cruach Mhalaig, you can still enjoy a fine view of the seascape.

By the public phone box at Mallaigvaig you will see a signpost showing the way back to Mallaig. This fine little path crosses the moorland above the village and finishes in an interesting little valley which takes you back all the way to the main road at the harbour.

All in all an interesting and rewarding walk in the company of gulls, curlews, lapwing and skylark.

Walk 5
CASTLE TIORAM
HIGHLAND
6 miles

Close to the A861 Lochailort to Salen road in Moidart, but offshore on a tidal island, stands the fourteenth century Castle Tioram of the MacDonalds of Clanranald. The island on which the castle stands is cut off from the mainland only at high tide, and access is easy at other times, although naturally care and an eye on the time are essential.

With high curtain walls and turreted keep the castle remains in a fair state of preservation, at least outwardly, and its imposing character gives a real indication of its grand prominence in times gone by. If you cross the sands you'll find that the old stone masons made it pentangular. This is because these craftsmen were expert in tailoring a building to fit its underlying crag.

The entrance of Castle Tioram faces north, looking towards Riskey. After passing through a small courtyard you will see a rough rocky terrace rising for about five feet to which roughly hewn steps offer access. The castle has a hall, a kitchen and a magnificent and typical musty dungeon. There is a lack of space, however, but that isn't untypical of castles of this type.

The building was put up in 1353 by the Lady Anne MacRuari, the divorced wife of John MacDonald the first Lord of the Isles. It was the son of that union, Ronald, who began the great Highland family known as Clanranald. These Lords of the Isles, as their name suggests, ruled both land and sea, a vast territory where most of the enemy attacks

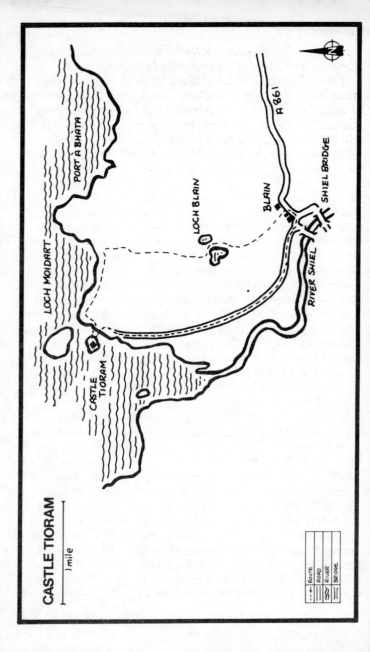

CASTLE TIORAM

1 mile

ROUTE
ROAD
RIVER
BRIDGE

PORT A BHÀTA

LOCH MOIDART

LOCH BLAIN

BLAIN

SHIEL BRIDGE

A 861

RIVER SHIEL

CASTLE TIORAM

came from the sea. It is perhaps for this reason that most of these seaboard castles have no walls facing the sea.

Castle Tioram was never taken by siege, but was once temporarily seized by the Duke of Argyll. He had been given a commission from the government of the time to harass Clanranald, and for five weeks his warships anchored around the waters close to the castle island. With the incumbents of the castle almost running out of food, Argyll, for no apparent reason, sailed off towards Ardnamurchan, and as soon as the galleys were out of sight Clanranald made good his escape. But Argyll was clever. As soon as Clanranald was out, he came back and took the empty castle. Clanranald hadn't fled very far though, and infuriated by the ruse, he gathered his clan and returned to the castle to murder each and every one of the invading Campbells.

The end of Castle Tioram came at the hands of its owner. At the first Jacobite Uprising in 1715, when Allen Dearg led his clan to fight for the Old Pretender, he justifiably feared that if he died in battle his ancient home would be seized by the Campbell of Argyll. He therefore gave orders that it should be put to fire, though he himself could not bear to watch it burn. Only the shell remains of this once imposing castle, a building rich in the history of the turbulent area. It's well worth a visit.

Park just north of Shiel Bridge and leave the main A861 by the minor road which runs down alongside the River Shiel. The river hereabouts runs broad and deep through a wooded valley, with the steep slopes of Beinn Gheur on your right-hand side.

After about two miles or so the river meets the waters of outer Loch Moidart, and shortly after this the road ends at the beach at Cul Doirlinn. In front of you, backed by the hills of Eilean Shona, stands the fourteenth-century castle.

As I mentioned earlier, access to the island of the castle depends very much on the state of the tides. I would recommend that you consult a book of tide tables, for I have known folk to become stranded overnight. It's not a long walk across, and you'll enjoy the sound of gulls, sandpipers,

Castle Tioram, a traditional Scottish keep on its tidal island.

lapwing and, possibly, ringed plover. I've seen this pretty little plover once or twice here and it's always a delight. The sound is also a good place for seeing herons, a bird that was once thought in these parts to bring bad luck.

Castle Tioram is imposing, with its backdrop of purple hills, rock and pebble. In many ways it's the archetypal highland castle, a place to be viewed to the sound of a bagpipe pibroch.

From Doirlinn, follow a footpath around the headlands above the loch to just before the point of Torr Port a Bhata. This is quite a rough track, but perfectly negotiable, and it is much more pleasant that taking the approach road back. Because it rises it offers some very fine west highland views with the castle itself as a frontispiece. From the point just before Torr Port a Bhata, another footpath climbs up and across the moors to Loch Blain, a place of wheeling gulls, shrill curlews and trumpeting lapwing. Stop for a bit and enjoy the music of the skylark before dropping down to the main road at Blain, just to the north of Shiel Bridge.

Walk 6
STEALL WATERFALL
HIGHLAND
3 miles

Of all the glens in the Western Highlands of Scotland, it's difficult to find one that compares in terms of ruggedness and splendour with Glen Nevis. Running south and then eastwards from Fort William, the glen curves faithfully around the humped contours of Ben Nevis, the highest mountain in Britain, offering a wide range of scenery from fertile pasture land to rocky, barren crags. A motor road runs down the length of the glen and where that road ends, at Polldubh, begins what has been described as the finest mile in Scotland, the path through the Nevis gorge to the wide green meadows of Steall.

At first the path is high above the torrent, offering fine views down the length of the Upper Glen Nevis, but soon it smoothes out alongside the chasm, a deep and tortuous channel where the thundering waters have eroded the rock into gouged pots and cauldrons.

You come out of the gorge to where the water of Nevis flows gently across the green meadows of Steall – a total contrast. The respite is only temporary though, for across the meadows, crashing down from the heights of the Garbhanach (The Rough Place) is the Grey Mare's Tail of the Steall Waterfall, cascading down an almost sheer crag for some 200 feet.

Steall, with its contrasting meadows and surrounding high craggy mountains, is a place of immense atmosphere. A small whitewashed cottage stands alone near the foot of the water-

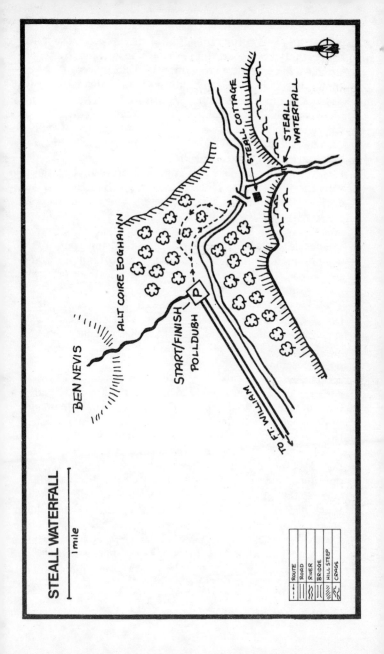

STEALL WATERFALL

1 mile

N

BEN NEVIS

ALLT COIRE EOGHAINN

START/FINISH
POLLDUBH

P

TO FT. WILLIAM

STEALL COTTAGE

STEALL
WATERFALL

- · -	ROUTE
|||	ROAD
≈≈	RIVER
⌇⌇	BRIDGE
///////	HILL STEEP
⋔⋔	CRAGS

fall, almost lost in the immensity of its surroundings. This former croft is now a mountaineering club hut, and to reach it you have to negotiate a low slung wire bridge over the river, an exciting challenge to mountaineers with loaded rucksacks.

The road south from Fort William runs up the glen and turns sharp left at Polldubh, to end two miles further on at a large car park. The track to Steall – which, incidentally, continues all the way to Dalwhinnie in the heart of Scotland – starts at the western end of the car park.

At the northern side of the car park an open and bare slope runs for 4,000 feet to the very summit of Ben Nevis at an angle of 35 degrees, reckoned to be the longest and steepest slope in Britain. I've walked it and can vouch for the fact that it certainly feels like it. To add to the drama of it, a stream crashes down its length, the Allt Coire Eoghainn, one of the most dramatic water slides in Scotland. It begins in the Coire Eoghainn high above and crashes down 1,250 feet in half a mile, white and foaming.

Follow the track out of the car park and soon you will be in the trees, just catching tantalising glimpses of the furious river below. After a few hundred yards you should be able to spot the white slash of the Steall Waterfall through the narrow V-shaped gorge.

The footpath climbs very little in its length and is well constructed. It soon bends to the right, following the contours of the gorge and offering long views down the length of upper Glen Nevis to the heights of Stob Ban and Mullach nan Coirean – a dramatic and impressive sight.

A few yards later and the view is gone. You are now in the bowels of the gorge itself, a gorge whose walls climb up high on either side of you, smooth water-cleansed walls which suggest that at one time the river would have been much, much higher. But in the course of the centuries the boiling action of the waters has worn their channel deeper and deeper, right down to the present level. Great gouts twist and churn and boil around gigantic boulders. Shallow caves have been gouged out of the rock walls at the side and much of the rock has worn as smooth as marble. Above you, the crags

Steall Waterfall, the great Grey Mare's Tail of Glen Nevis.

glisten black, and close in on either side of you.

And then, suddenly and without warning, the scene changes dramatically. A great boulder appears to bar the way, but is easily crossed without any difficulty. A flat and grassy meadow extends away in front of you as far as the next bend in the river, and above it the scene is dominated by the great waterfall of Steall. Such is the contrast of this scene with the violence and noise of the gorge that it takes several seconds to register.

A footpath runs across the left side of the meadow, but if you are only walking as far as the Steall Waterfall you are better walking on the grass alongside the now lethargic river. Follow it for a couple of hundred yards to the wire hawser bridge which leads over to the cottage. Take care on the bridge, for the river below often has a swift undercurrent despite its benevolent look.

Opposite you, looking eastwards, the Steall Glen continues on its way to Loch Trieg and some wild, remote country. The high hills of the Aonachs, Grey Corries and Mamores surround you (over 40 3,000 foot summits are accessible from here), and on a clear day you may see the summit slopes of Ben Nevis towering high above the gorge.

You can return to the car park at Polldubh by the same route, or take a more interesting, if a little more energetic, way. Retrace your steps to where the slow moving river enters the chasm, and instead of crossing the boulders back to the gorge path turn immediately right and follow a faint track steeply uphill. As you climb the path becomes more obvious and it begins to zig-zag to make the climbing a bit easier.

After climbing a few hundred feet – which has the effect of opening up infinitely greater views all round – the path continues more or less parallel to the one deep down in the gorge, and eventually drops down amid rowan, birch and oak to regain the original path just a few hundred yards short of the car park.

Walk 7
THE LOST VALLEY OF GLENCOE
HIGHLAND
3 miles

Glencoe is a place of haunting beauty. Certainly not a pretty place, or scenically attractive as, say, Loch Lomond-side. Rather, Glencoe has an austerity that, particularly in bad weather, can be almost frightening. Its scenery is on the grand scale and the car-borne tourist is both dwarfed and humbled by the landscape around him.

The objective for this walk lies in the tight clench of surrounding ridges and peaks – a lost valley which provides a haven not only for the walker and climber but for wildlife as well. It is a marvellous place to lie and watch the herds of red deer wander down from the tops, grazing peacefully on the lush grass of the valley basin. In this lost valley I have also spotted a ptarmigan – the mountain grouse, the Arctic species which turns from its usual mottled grey to pure white during the winter months.

If you are lucky, you'll also see in this secluded and very special place eagle, buzzard, and possibly a peregrine falcon. Chaffinches predominate in the birch woods at the lower end of the valley, but higher up you are likely to hear the harsh clacking of a ring ouzel, the mountain blackbird.

As you drive into the jaws of Glencoe from the south, you are immediately aware that this is a pass of note. The road winds on before you, passing one or two small farms amongst tracings of greenery. A loch at the far end of the glen, Loch Achtriochtan, affords some relief from the austere setting, and beyond it the sea begins at Loch Leven.

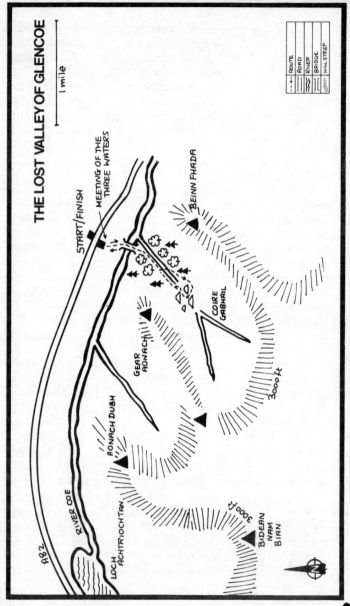

On your right-hand side an imposing mountain barrier seals the glen from the north. It's a great wall, torn and riven by scree runs, narrow gullies which more often than not hold the remains of the winter's snow, even well into July. Frequently the top of this wall is capped by cloud, but if you are lucky enough to arrive there on a clear day you'll notice that the top of this great ridge is crooked, jagged and rough, torn by pinnacles, spires and gullies. This is the Aonach Eagach Ridge, the Notched Ridge, and it offers mountaineers and scramblers a challenging walk along its three mile switch-backed crest.

While the Aonach Eagach creates a continuous barrier along the north side of the glen, the south side is more complex. One great mountain, the highest in the old county of Argyll, is Bidean nan Bian, and it throws out three great fingers into the confines of the pass. Each of these ridges protrudes into the glen in great rock buttresses, and viewed from the top of the glen it's easy to see why they are called the Three Sisters of Glencoe. These are in the most part sheer rock faces; one of them, Aonach Dubh, shows a vertical slit high on its north face. This is Ossian's Cave, named after the bardic warrior son of Finn McCuil, or Fingal as he is generally known in Scotland.

In between these great buttresses lie huge scalloped glacial cirques, known in Scotland as corries. One of them, lying between Beinn Fhada and Gear Aonach, can't be seen very clearly from the road, and is known as the Coire Ghabail, or the Lost Valley.

Legend has it that the MacDonalds of Glencoe, who once lived in the lower stretches of Glencoe, used to hide stolen cattle up here, where they couldn't be spotted by passing government troops. Like most of the highland clans at the time, the MacDonalds were known freebooters and cattle reivers. They were, in fact, a considerable thorn in the flesh of the government at the time, and they consistently refused to pay allegiance to the king of the day, William. Eventually their clan chief, MacIan, did travel south to pay homage to the king, but he arrived too late to prevent orders being sent

High and hidden, the lost valley of Glencoe was once used to hide stolen cattle.

from the government to the garrison stationed at Inverlochy, now known as Fort William, ten miles north of Glencoe. These orders were to 'put all to the sword under ninety'.

The Massacre of Glencoe is remembered even today, not so much as an act of discipline by the government, nor as an inter-clan feud, but because of the way the orders were carried out. Pretending that the garrison at Fort William was overfull, the captain of the regiment who had been given the orders – a Campbell, as were many of the soldiers – told the MacDonalds that the soldiers had to be billeted with the Glencoe families. One night, under cover of dark, the alarm was raised; the soldiers rose and murdered their hosts. Thus the age-old custom of highland hospitality was breached, and the clan Campbell has never been forgiven.

The Lost Valley, then, is well worth a visit in the glen of history. To start the walk, leave the main A82 at the Meeting of the Three Waters and take the obvious footpath down to the gorge formed by the River Coe. A footbridge crosses the river and its rocky gorge, and a footpath climbs up from it to follow the banks of the Allt Coire Gabhail. The path steepens here and there but take your time and enjoy the views back down the length of the glen towards Loch Achtriochtan.

Higher up, the path runs through a deep cleft among birch trees; a marvellous place to be in spring and autumn. Take care as you follow the path now as it waves in and out between rocky outcrops, and eventually crosses the burn to a gravelly path which takes you above the trees to the breathtaking splendour of the upper corrie.

Here lies the great green meadow of the Lost Valley, hemmed in by the steep-sided and jagged ridges of Bidean nam Bian, a direct contrast to the rocky tree-clad route we have just followed. It's to this secluded place that the Macdonalds of Glencoe brought their cattle to graze on the green meadows undisturbed.

Take a walk up the half a mile of the meadow where the stream runs underground, and enjoy the solitude of it all.

Return to the A82 by the same path, but look back up behind you as you go to appreciate just how hidden the valley is.

Walk 8
DUN DO LAMH–FORT OF THE TWO HANDS
HIGHLAND
3 miles

From near the village of Laggan in the Badenoch district of the Scottish Highlands, there runs a very old road. This highway was built by the navvies and soldiers under the command of General Wade during the eighteenth century in an attempt to increase communications within the 'wild highlands'. It was thought that by having decent roads, regiments of soldiers could quickly be brought into troubled areas where the highland clans were becoming rebellious, and thus it came to pass that the Corrieyairack Pass, from Laggan to Fort Augustus at the head of Loch Ness, was built.

Close to the start of the road, high above the Spey dam, where the waters of the River Spey have been harnessed to give hydro-electric power, there stands a conical forested hill. It commands an important position where two glens meet at what is the beginning of the Spey Valley. One glen holds the Corrieyairack Pass and the infant River Spey. Rising high in the Monadh Liath mountains, the Spey roars down in tumultuous fashion for its first few mlies, before it is calmed down and slowed by the flat Spey valley at Laggan.

Running almost parallel with the Corrieyairack Pass, separated from it by an outlier of the great Creag Meagaidh range, is the glen of Strathmashie which runs down from Loch Laggan, an old and important route from the west.

Assuming that General Wade built the Corrieyairack road because the line of it already provided a route from the north, we can begin to understand how this conical hill took on some

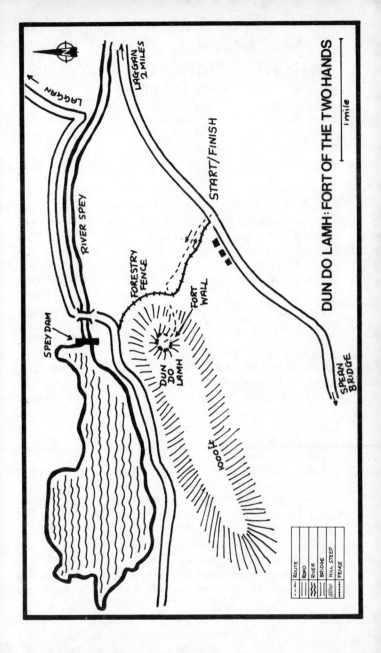

DUN DO LAMH: FORT OF THE TWO HANDS

LAGGAN

LAGGAN 2 MILES

START/FINISH

SPEAN BRIDGE

RIVER SPEY

FORESTRY FENCE

FORT WALL

DUN DO LAMH

SPEY DAM

1000 ft

N

1 mile

| ROUTE |
| ROAD |
| RIVER |
| BRIDGE |
| HILL STEEP |
| FENCE |

great importance in ancient days. In short, it provided a look-out above routes leading from the north, the west and the east. With high hills barring the way to the south there was obviously no fear of attack from that direction.

At the top of this conical hill, almost forming a crown around its summit cone, are the remains of an Iron Age fort – the objective for this walk. It is known as the Dun do Lamh, or the Fort of the Two Hands.

This fort is held to be one of the most perfect relics of a British stronghold of its kind. Standing 600 feet above the valley it is a superb viewpoint, and the extent of its remains seems to indicate that it was a fairly sizeable structure at one time. The dimensions of the dun, or fort, within its surrounding walls, are 420 feet in length, 250 feet wide at its western end, 110 feet wide at the centre and 75 feet wide at its eastern extremity. The wall appears to have varied considerably in its height, and it is now from 2 to 5 feet in height and 14 feet in thickness. At the western side the wall was 17 feet thick, and in the north-west corner no less than 25 feet thick, that being the most vulnerable and exposed part of the hill. It is believed that the wall hereabouts may well have been about 20 feet in height.

Like most of these ancient ruins there is no evidence to suggest that the walls were built with lime or cement, and indeed there is evidence to suggest that the remains of the fort have been vitrified, that is the rocks and stones have been fused together by intense heat; whether done on purpose by setting fire to the fort, or whether a fire was caused by hostilities no-one seems to know.

A few years ago a large heap of iron slag, or cinder, was discovered together with a large circular hole faced with stone and filled with ashes and charcoal. This was thought to have been used for smelting iron. It was also thought that the heaps of cinder showed evidence of much greater heat than could have been produced by a smith's forge.

The tradition locally is that the dun was built and used by Fingalian warriors, the tribe of fair-haired giants led by Finn McCuil. Another hill which bears their name, Tom na

Dun do Lamh, the Fort of the Two Hands, an ancient iron age structure with spectacular views.

Feinne, stands just a few miles down the Spey.

The fort appears to have had two approaches, one on the north side and one on the south. Our approach is through the forestry plantation on the south side. Unfortunately the approach from the north side is now largely covered with trees, but is nevertheless very steep and rugged. It's thought that access by the north was via a straight steep gully where large boulders could have been sent crashing down on unwelcome visitors.

Leave your car near the forestry houses on the main A86 Laggan to Spean Bridge road, about two miles south of Laggan, and take the forestry track that leads north-west away from the houses towards Spey Dam. A few hundred yards along this track another track leads off to your left, through a forestry gate and into the plantation. Go through the gate and follow the track as it climbs higher through the plantation. It zig-zags its way high on the hill and soon turns back on itself to lead towards the hill on which Dun do Lamh stands.

Where the track stops, a small footpath begins, bearing off leftwards up through the heather at the side of the tree plantation. This path follows the watercourse of a small stream before winding off to the right, to go through the trees and follow a final rough causeway up by the side of one of the fort walls. At the top you'll find a rough shelter (made in recent years) and you'll be able to trace the outline of the fort.

It's best to return to your car the same way, although the more adventurous can easily find a route down towards the Spey Dam on the north side of the hill through the trees. Return to your car by the forestry track that wends its way round the foot of the hill.

Walk 9
WHERE THE FESHIE MEETS THE SPEY
HIGHLAND
3 miles

The village of Kincraig nestles in a sheltered position at the north end of Loch Insh in the old district of Badenoch. Kincraig is a relatively new name, for at the beginning of the century the village was known as Boat of Insh. Here, where the mighty River Spey flows out of Loch Insh, a small ferry boat plied, and once carried Queen Victoria herself across the swift waters.

The Spey is one of Scotland's longest rivers, rising high in the Monadh Liath mountains, and tumbling down 3,000 feet in a matter of 90 miles. Her initial course is tumultuous, but as she enters the broad valley after Newtonmore she grows languid and meandering, so much so that often she floods her banks hereabouts and has created the large fenlands known today as Insh Marshes, now managed as a bird reserve. After the Marshes, she flows into Loch Insh and is then squeezed out at the other end to continue her way to the North Sea.

A mile or so north-east of Kincraig, another river makes its way to lower ground. The River Feshie rises high in the Cairngorms and makes a hurried descent down the length of Glen Feshie, one of the most attractive in the eastern highlands. The confluence of these two rivers, the slow moving Spey and the turbulent Feshie, can often, especially after heavy rain, make an exciting prospect.

As you approach the point where the two rivers meet, it sometimes seems that the Spey is running the wrong way. When the Feshie is running high and swollen it forces the

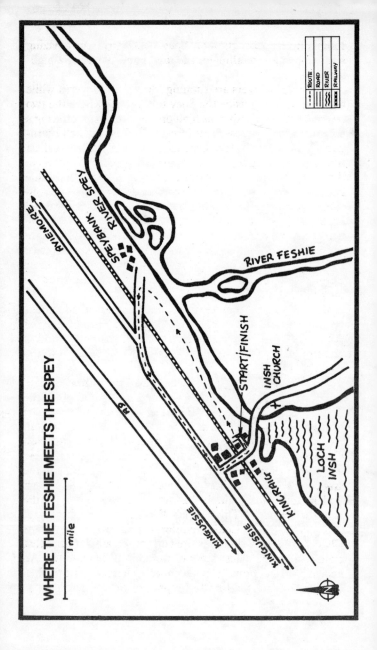

WHERE THE FESHIE MEETS THE SPEY

1 mile

AVIEMORE

SPEYBANK RIVER SPEY

RIVER FESHIE

START/FINISH

INSH CHURCH

KINCRAIG

LOCH INSH

KINGUSSIE

KINGUSSIE

····	ROUTE
	ROAD
⌇⌇⌇	RIVER
✕✕✕	RAILWAY

comparatively slow-running Spey backwards, an amazing sight showing something of the might and power of a highland river.

Even if both rivers are running low, it's well worth while taking a walk alongside the Spey to this spot where the two rivers meet. The path runs high on the river bank offering a panoramic view across great forests towards the high Cairngorms. On a clear day, Braeriach, Britain's third highest mountain, will grace the scene with its massive presence, dwarfing the other mountains around it. The River Feshie runs down through forests of conifer and widens out considerably just before running into the Spey. This has created large gravel banks and sand banks, ideal places for watching heron or if you're really lucky, spotting otters. Buzzards are often seen spiralling in the air thermals and more than once I've seen osprey fish here, following the course of the Spey or Feshie using their magnificent eyesight to locate trout or salmon in the water below.

Kincraig is on the A9 Perth to Inverness road, about midway between Kingussie and Aviemore. Turn off the old A9 road into the village and drive down the road under a railway bridge. Park near the telephone box adjacent to the post office.

Walk past the post office, back towards the railway bridge, but before you reach it you'll find a road turning off to the right, signposted to Speybank. This is the road we want: tarmac for a hundred yards or so it then becomes a footpath passing through some attractive woods of birch and oak. Once past the houses the path takes on a fine character, rising high above the waters of the Spey. At the first opening in the trees you'll catch the first good view, back towards the loch and its tiny white church that sits on a promontory at the head of the loch. This is Insh Kirk of the Presbytery of Abernethy, but in Celtic tradition it's known as the Swans Chapel. This tiny church is sited on consecrated ground that claims to be the oldest place of worship in the country. An ancient bell sits proudly in the church, claimed to be the bell of St Adamnan, the first biographer of St Columba.

Where the Feshie meets the Spey, the scenic confluence of two highland rivers.

An ancient Celtic tale, the Swan Children of Lir, tells of the King of Lir – an area in Ireland in the third century. His three children, two girls and a boy, were known throughout all Erin for their fair beauty. When the king's wife died, he married again, but this wife was something of a witch. Passionately jealous of the children, she turned them into swans, destined to fly for 300 years between Scotland and Ireland. One of the places these swan-children visited was Loch Insh, where they were summoned to worship by a monk who rang a bell for them. The monk was St Adamnan, the bell said to be the very one hanging in the church today.

It's a quaint story, but there's an interesting link with the present. Loch Insh, and nearby Insh Marshes, are today one of the principle wintering places in Scotland for whooper swans. In late autumn, five or six hundred of these swans fly south from Greenland and Iceland and take up temporary residence here until the spring. So you can still hear the sweet bugling of the swan children as they fly up and down the Spey during the winter months.

Carry on down the footpath, climbing one or two steep parts. These hills are not long, and you are well rewarded for your trouble when you reach the top, for the views become better the further you walk along the path, and the higher you rise.

At the highest point on the path you'll find a couple of wooden benches, and it's well worthwhile stopping for a bit and enjoying the view. Below you the waters of the Feshie crash into the Spey, slashing a great gap in the vast forests that fill the valley between you and the rising Cairngorms.

Once you have feasted on this view, carry on the path for a couple of hundred yards. The path stops at a gate which you go through, and turn immediately left, to follow a tarmac lane across the railway line, and after about half a mile back onto the old A9 road. Turn left onto the road and follow it back into Kincraig village.

Walk 10
LANDSEER'S BOTHY
HIGHLAND
6½ miles

The name Glen Feshie is a corruption of the Gaelic Gleann Feisidh, which means Glen of the Fairy Stream, an attractive name for what is possibly the most attractive of all the fine glens in the Cairngorms area. The beauty of the glen attracted the Victorian artist Edwin Landseer, and he spent several holidays in the area, sketching and painting the evocative highland scenery. One of his most famed paintings, 'Stag at Bay', was inspired by the herds of red deer stags which often came into the glen when he was living in a small hut near the present Glen Feshie Lodge.

There were, in fact, several huts in the area, and one of them, the one which is thought to have been used by Landseer, is still standing and is used as a bothy – an open shelter for walkers. It is owned by the Glen Feshie Estate and is maintained to a very high standard by the Mountain Bothies Association. It is known as Ruigh-aiteachain or sheiling of the juniper flats.

The bothy is a solid building containing two large rooms and a floored attic which is normally used for sleeping accommodation. One of the rooms contains a large stone fireplace, and for years walkers and climbers have enjoyed the glow and crackle of wood fires as they spend long winter nights in the bothy. One can almost visualise Landseer himself settled in front of the fire, his paint and easel before him, putting shape to the haunting highland images that he so obviously enjoyed.

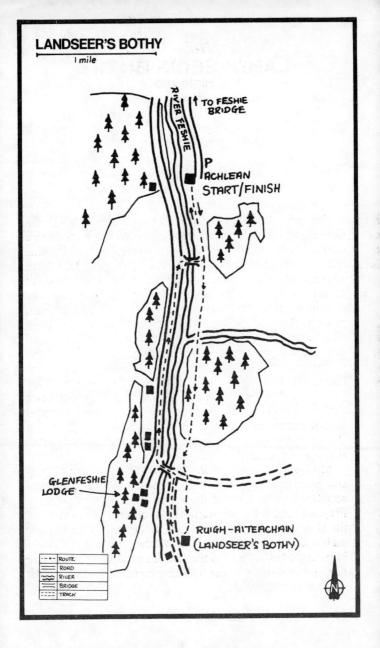

Close by stands a ruin of another hut and all that is left of that is a stone chimney. Until the 1930s, you could see a fresco of several red deer sketched on the wall above the fireplace, drawn of course by Edwin Landseer.

The spot in which the bothy stands is a particularly fine place, well sheltered from the stormy blasts by ancient Caledonian pines and clumps of juniper. High heather-clad hills surround the glen on three sides and in the autumn the place comes alive with the primeval sounds of rutting stags and the clamouring of skeins of migrating geese which use the glen as a migration corridor through the high Cairngorms.

Landseer's Bothy can be reached by a fine low level walk which begins at the farm steading of Achlean, five miles south of Feshiebridge on the B970 road. There is adequate car parking on rough ground at the side of the road, but vehicles are requested not to use Achlean itself as a turning area.

From Achlean, there is a majestic view down to the head of Glen Feshie, where tall hills appear to form a great headwall to the open glen. To your left a rough path, locally known as the Foxhunter's Path, leaves the low ground to climb high into the hills of the Moine Mor, or the Great Moss, a high-level area of peat hag and rolling hills, a favourite haunt of the red deer and of such Arctic birds as the dotterel and ptarmigan.

Take the obvious path south from the farmhouse at Achlean and follow it onto the wide river flats close to the River Feshie. There are some fine bathing pools in the river hereabouts and many a warm summer afternoon can be spent in the 'natural jacuzzis' where the river pours through the granite rocks and boulders. Follow the path south until you pass by the footbridge over the river. (You'll cross this bridge later on your return journey.) The path now leaves the river flats and climbs slightly onto a long heather ridge.

In just over half a mile you'll have to cross the waters of the Allt Garblach – a narrow stream which issues from the great cleft of Coire Garblach on your left – and climb a stile into the

Landseer's Bothy, once used by the Victorian artist, Edwin Landseer.

forest of Coille an Torr, the Wood of the Hillock, a pleasant mixture of broadleafed trees, modern conifer and old Caledonian pines. Look out for the brightly coloured crossbills, known as the Scottish parrot, whose crossed beaks are used for prising the seeds from pine cones. Members of the titmouse family, particularly the rare crested tit, can be seen here too, particularly near and on the old pines.

Follow the path through the forest to its southern extremity, where another stile allows you to cross the fence to the continuation of the path which now runs alongside the fast flowing River Feshie.

Keep following the path, which soon turns into a fairly wide track, from where it has crossed the footbridge just below the stalkers' houses on the other side of the river. Soon the bothy will come into sight through the pine trees and juniper bushes.

The return to Achlean is considerably easier, much of it on a rough tarmac road which is closed to motor traffic. The road can be reached by crossing the footbridge over the river, just below the buildings at Carnachuin. Follow the road northwards for just under two miles and then cross over a footbridge back to the Achlean side of the river. Pick up the track again for the final walk back to Achlean.

This flat area to the south of Achlean was once used as a gathering place of cattle drovers. The cattle, small black and shaggy, would graze on the lush pastures beside the Feshie while the drovers met, harangued, bargained and no doubt fought. This was the Glen Feshie cattle tryst, the highland fair that preceded the better-known and more recent trysts at Crieff and Falkirk, much further south.

It's difficult now to imagine the scene, and it's equally difficult to understand the local legends of the Daoine Sith, the fairy folk. And yet people have spoken of foxgloves bending in the air when there was no breath of wind, and, on reaching them, they no longer stirred but others did further along the way. Keep your eyes open . . .

Walk 11
LOCH AN EILEAN – LOCH OF THE ISLAND
HIGHLAND
7 miles

Loch an Eilean, with its island castle, is one of the best-known and most loved beauty spots in the Highlands of Scotland. For the author, it is the most picturesque loch in Scotland, with its backdrop of heather clad mountains, ancient pine forest and craggy skyline. It lies like a jewel amid the splendour of the Rothiemurchus Forest, a priceless natural asset of ancient Caledonian pine which once offered shelter to bears, wolves, lynx and great elk. Nowadays, particularly around Loch an Eilean, the naturalist can enjoy the sight and sounds of crossbills, crested tits, siskin, greenshank and if he is lucky, the exciting view of an osprey diving for trout.

Loch an Eilean's chief claim to fame is a castle which is built on a tiny island just off the north-western shore. This ancient keep dates from the fourteenth century and was once a stronghold of the mighty Norman family of Comyns, the Lords of Badenoch. It is also thought that the castle was once used by the Wolf of Badenoch, one Alexander Stewart, the bastard son of Robert II of Scotland. This rogue gained his nickname after burning down Elgin Cathedral, the abbot of which had criticised him for having an affair. For his troubles he was excommunicated from the Catholic Church and more or less outlawed.

Today the castle is a ruin, grown over with ivy and birch trees. It faces the north-western shore of the loch with a blank wall which contains one open door. There are stepping stones

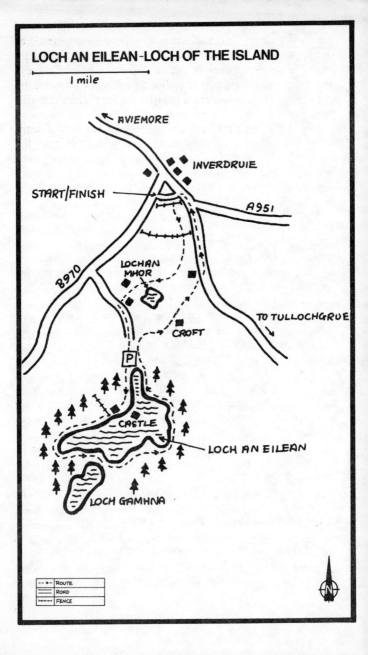

LOCH AN EILEAN-LOCH OF THE ISLAND

I mile

AVIEMORE

INVERDRUIE

START/FINISH

A951

B970

LOCHAN MHOR

TO TULLOCHGRUE

CROFT

P

CASTLE

LOCH AN EILEAN

LOCH GAMHNA

ROUTE
ROAD
FENCE

N

out to the island, but these can only be seen in periods of severe drought, when the level of the loch water is extremely low. The castle ruins once gave a home to a pair of ospreys who built their eyrie on the walls, but constant attention by egg collectors harassed them greatly and they left earlier this century.

There is a car park at the north end of Loch an Eilean, which offers easy access to a nature trail which encircles the loch (three miles), but if time is available it is far better to link the walk around the loch with a longer walk through Rothiemurchus from Inverdruie, one and a half miles south-east of Aviemore on the A951 Glenmore road.

At Inverdruie, the Rothiemurchus Estate Ranger Service have an Information Centre which would be well worth visiting before setting out for Loch an Eilean.

Across the road from the Information Centre, there is a triangle of roads formed at the junction of the B970 and the A951. On the south side of this triangle an obvious gate gives access through some trees onto moorland. Follow this path for just over half a mile until it is joined by another, wider, track coming in from the left. Continue on this combined track for about 500 yards until you reach the banks of Lochan Mhor, the Big Lochan. This very scenic spot is a water fowl sanctuary where such species as tufted duck, little grebe and mallard can be seen in season. In early summer the edges of the loch are covered in water lilies.

Continue along the track in a westerly direction through heather moorland. This is a good place for spotting roe deer, the smaller deer of the forests, and, in winter, red deer driven down from the high tops by the wind and snow to search for food within the forest.

Soon you will pass a small cottage on your right, and then another on your left. Go through the cottage gate here, remembering to close it behind you, and turn left onto a minor public road. Follow this for just over half a mile to Loch an Eilean.

A nature trail runs around the loch for three miles – easy walking in magnificent surroundings. Much of the forest is

Loch an Eilean, arguably the most attractive loch in Scotland.

old Caledonian pine, gnarled red trees which seem to characterise this part of the highlands. Look out for the birds of the pine forest, and for red squirrels who live here in great numbers. If you're really lucky you might even spot a pine marten, a creature who is re-colonising this part of Speyside after being almost extinct.

At the head of the loch, another narrow trail strikes off to the right. If you have time this is worth following, for it will take you around the small but beautiful Loch Gamhna, the Loch of the Stirks, or young cattle. This reed-fringed loch is seldom visited, and offers a tranquility rarely found in busy Speyside.

Continue with your walk around Loch an Eilean back to the car park at the northern end of the loch. There is another Information Centre here which also sells postcards, sweets and soft drinks.

For the return to Inverdruie continue down the public

road from the car park for about 150 yards. Take the rough road that leads off to the right up a short rise and follow this on past some rough pasture land. There will probably be cattle grazing here, for Rothiemurchus is well known in farming circles for its beef herds.

Soon you will pass a large house, called the Croft, on your right, and another one will be seen through the trees on your left. After a distance another house, Black Park, will appear on your left and here you join the public road which has come down from the right from Whitewell. Follow this road back to Inverdruie.

Walk 12
THE LAIRIG GHRU VIEW
HIGHLAND
8 or 10½ miles

The pass of the Lairig Ghru, the Gloomy Pass, is one of the classic high-level passes in Scotland. It cuts through the great massif of the Cairngorms, a great cleft caused by glaciation, with the bulk of Ben MacDhui on one side and Braeriach on the other – Britain's second and third highest hills respectively. The route itself, from Coylumbridge near Aviemore through the Cairngorms' heartland to Braemar in the south, is some 30 miles in length and rises to a height of over two and a half thousand feet. Such a walk is, of course, outwith the scope of this book, but a superb walk can be enjoyed through the magnificent forest of Rothiemurchus, up through the ancient remains of the Caledonian Pine Forest to the mouth of the Lairig Ghru where there are superb views back over the forest, across Glenmore towards the rising swell of the Monadh Liath hills.

Rothiemurchus is the name of the parish which lies between the River Spey and the summits of the high Cairngorms. Because of the variety of landforms contained in the estate the landscape passes from low-lying fields and hard woods around the fast-flowing rivers, through open moorland ablaze with purple heather in the autumn, through mixed woodland, forestry plantations and the remnants of the Caledonian Pine Forest. Beyond this swell the great rounded domes of the Cairngorms.

The early history of the area was varied and colourful, and its ownership passed through the hands of Comyns, Gor-

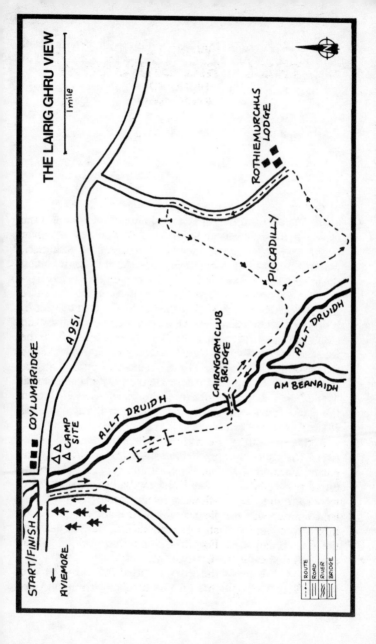

THE LAIRIG GHRU VIEW

N

1 mile

START/FINISH

AVIEMORE

COYLUMBRIDGE

A951

CAMP SITE

ALLT DRUIDH

CAIRNGORM CLUB BRIDGE

ALLT DRUIDH

AM BEARNAIDH

PICCADILLY

ROTHIEMURCHUS LODGE

ROUTE
ROAD
RIVER
BRIDGE

dons, Shaws and McIntoshes before settling in those of Patrick Grant of Muckerach, the second son of the Chief of Grant in 1580.

Our walk begins at Coylumbridge, about two miles south-east of Aviemore on the A951. A lay-by at the side of the road provides parking space. Take the footpath which runs alongside the camping ground and which is signposted 'The Lairig Ghru'.

Right away the character of Rothiemurchus imposes on you. You'll pass a small cottage on the left and from then on there is no more habitation until Rothiemurchus Lodge, owned by the Joint Services, many miles away. Already you are in rich woodland, with a deep and luxuriant undergrowth of bracken, birch scrub and juniper. The red deer are comparatively few on this side of the Cairngorms, and the undergrowth has a good chance to regenerate without being chewed away.

After a short distance you'll come to a fork in the path. Take the left path past a large stone cairn which indicates the Lairig Ghru. Cross the clearing with dense juniper bushes on your right before crossing a stream and heading back into the woodlands. Another stream is crossed by an old railway sleeper, and the next mile or so is through a fairly young conifer plantation. Compare the closely planted commercial conifers with the next stretch of the walk, ancient Caledonian Pine, and you'll realise just how far removed from a natural environment our forests have become.

As you leave the young plantation behind, the first tantalising glimpses of the higher hills come into view: the great craggy cliffs of Luchers Crag, or Creag an Leth-Choin, forming one of the jaws of the Lairig Ghru and the Sron Lairig ridge of Braeriach forming the other. In front, the conical shape of Carn Elrig dominates the scene.

What an area this is for wild life. If you're lucky you'll spot roe deer, red deer and squirrels, and if very lucky possibly wild cat, fox, and perhaps even a pine marten, making a comeback to this area after many years absence. Stop at the Iron Bridge across the river where the Allt Druidh and the

Lairig Ghru: the view from one of Scotland's best-known mountain passes.

Am Beanaidh meet and see if you can spot dippers, those dapper little birds that dive into the waters of these fast-flowing streams and search for food on the river beds. You'll recognise it by its dark appearance and white bib. Cross the bridge and continue along the footpath, through some open ground where there lie some ancient ruins, and around a bend to the meeting of the ways.

This is the spot known locally as Piccadilly on account of the paths going in various directions. Our route lies upwards, past the signpost which points you in the direction of the Lairig Ghru and Braemar. This is a superb path, climbing steadily up through the pines. Notice how the pines become shorter and more stunted as you climb. Gradually we leave the forest habitat behind and enter an area of glacial moraine, the rubbish churned up and left by the great glaciers as they carved their way through these big hills. Continue on the path with the Lairig Ghru pass immediately in front. On an overcast day you'll understand why it was called the Gloomy Pass. The sides are steep and scree clad, the very epitome of a mountain pass.

In a short time you'll reach a signpost pointing out Rothiemurchus Lodge, off to the left, so now is a good time to stop for a break and enjoy the view. From here you can gaze across the canopy of trees towards the distant Monadh Liath hills and those beyond. On a fine day Ben Wyvis, beyond Inverness, stands out clearly.

If you wish to keep the total walk length to about eight miles, then turn back at this point and retrace your steps. If you have the time and energy to continue for an extra two and a half miles, there is a detour which you can now follow past Rothiemurchus Lodge.

The path round towards Rothiemurchus Lodge is often muddy after bouts of rain, but the worst of it can be avoided. Rothiemurchus Lodge is a training school run by the Joint Services, and a Land Rover track leads downhill from it back towards Glenmore. It's a typical Joint Services track, built as though to take tank regiments rather than the occasional Land Rover. Aesthetically it's totally displeasing and unnecessary but you don't have to suffer it for long, for after a mile or so you turn back into the forest over a stile in the deer fence on the left, and back down the track to Piccadilly. From there, follow your earlier track back down through Rothiemurchus to Coylumbridge.

Walk 13
LOCHAN UAINE – THE GREEN LOCHAN
HIGHLAND
4½ miles

The Pass of Ryvoan, near Glenmore in the Cairngorms, was the thieves' route of old, part of the ancient Rathad nan Meirlach. This was the escape route of cattle thieves who would come through from the west on quiet byways, and in the darkness of night would raid the rich pasture lands of Moray.

In the heart of the pass lies Lochan Uaine, the Green Lochan, whose greenish-blue waters are so translucent that you can see the bottom of it. Local legend maintains that the water of the lochan has this colour because the local fairy folk wash their clothes in it and dance around the hill, Creag nan Gall, the Hill of the Stranger, just behind it.

The colour may be due partly to the contrast with the salmon pink screes behind the lochan, and partly to the reflection of the pine trees which surround the lochan. Whatever causes the strange hue, fairy folk or not, Lochan Uaine is a delightful destination for a short walk and perhaps a picnic. Its position in the middle of the Ryvoan Pass has attracted many famous artists and photographers, with the lochan hemmed in by scree runnelled crags on either side, the forests beyond, and looming over it all, the splendid backdrop of the Cairngorm mountains themselves. The pass is, in fact, a very good example of a glacial overflow channel, and the lochan has no visible outlet but drains below ground to the streams which run down to Loch Morlich in Glenmore.

If you gaze north through the pass, the gable end of a small

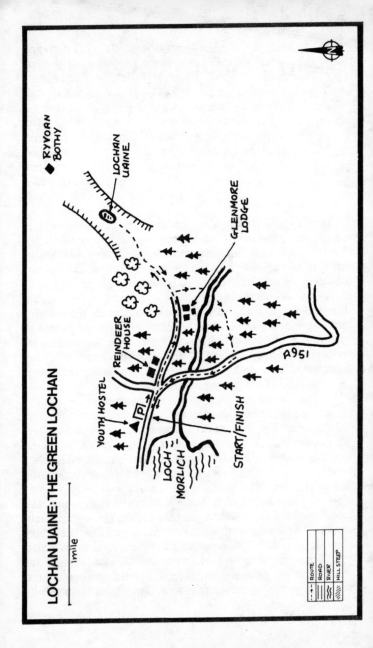

LOCHAN UAINE: THE GREEN LOCHAN

1 mile

◆ RYVOAN BOTHY

LOCHAN UAINE

GLENMORE LODGE

A951

REINDEER HOUSE

YOUTH HOSTEL

P

START/FINISH

LOCH MORLICH

ROUTE
ROAD
RIVER
HILL STEP

building can be seen on the horizon about half a mile away. This is the Ryvoan bothy, a shelter for walkers which was once a farm. Its original name was Ruighe a'Bhothain, meaning the shieling of the cottage. It is maintained by the Mountain Bothies Association and is in a very good state of repair, and is well worth the extra walk to visit it. The bothy is also the starting point for a track which runs to the summit of Meall a'Bhuachaille, a fine hill of 2,654 feet which offers superlative views across Glenmore to the main Cairngorm massif. It should be noted however that this is a hill walk, however straightforward, and it's quite a long pull to the top for those unaccustomed to mountain walking.

The tiny village of Glenmore consists of a Youth Hostel, a shop, a campsite, a watersports centre on the shores of Loch Morlich, and some forestry houses. There is a car park on the main road just below the Youth Hostel which is ideal as the starting point for the Lochan Uaine walk.

A monument in the car park commemorates Norwegian Commandos who trained in the Cairngorms during the Second World War. The high tops of the Cairngorms have a distinct Arctic climate and are well suited to the training of personnel involved in Arctic combat. Many of those who trained here formed strong links with the area, and even today those links are celebrated at frequent intervals.

Leave the car park and follow the main road for a short distance eastwards. Take the road that comes in from the left; after a few yards this road branches into three; you want the right-hand branch, signposted to Glenmore Lodge. This takes you along below what is locally known as the Reindeer House, a white building with a large fenced-in paddock behind it.

Back in 1947, Mikel Utsi, a Swedish Lapp, saw the Cairngorms through a late April snowstorm and immediately thought 'reindeer country!' He believed that he could reintroduce reindeer to the Scottish highlands, a species which had become extinct in Britain hundreds of years ago. After many initial difficulties he succeeded, and the reindeer herd on Cairngorm is now thriving and is being successfully

Lochan Uaine, the Green Lochan of the Glenmore fairy folk.

farmed. During the summer months, visitors can accompany herdsmen as they go out to feed the herd on the lower slopes of Cairngorm.

In about three quarters of a mile you come to the end of the tarmac road, just past the Norwegian-style buildings of Glenmore Lodge, the National Mountaineering Centre. This centre is run by the Scottish Sports Council and is recognised as being the top outdoor education establishment in the country.

A good forestry track now takes you through the forest, crossing a concrete bridge over the narrow Allt na Feith Duibhe and into the entrance of the pass. An interesting observation here is the distinct difference between commercially planted conifers on your right, and the more open and scenically attractive native Caledonian forest on your left. The gnarled pines clothe the slopes of Creag Loisgte and lower down mix with a rich carpet of heather and juniper. The colours, particularly in late August and September when the heather blooms deep purple, are stunning.

The Lochan itself is not seen from the track until you

arrive next to it, when it presents itself with something of a surprise, cradled in its heather-ringed hollow. Stand by the edge of the water and try out the echo against the opposite shores, reflected back from the red screes of Creag nan Gall.

To return to Glenmore retrace your steps for about three quarters of a mile to just before the bridge over the Allt na Feith Duibhe. Another forestry track turns off to the left and offers a fine forest walk back to Glenmore rather than retracing your steps. Follow this track for about one and a quarter miles, ignoring the various tracks which branch off in other directions, and you will be brought out onto the A951 Cairngorm road south of the Glenmore car park.

Walk 14
LINN OF DEE
GRAMPIAN
7 miles

The Linn of Dee is a rocky gorge, about 150 yards long but only a few wide, through which the entire content of the River Dee has to pass. The Dee itself is born high on the Braeriach plateau several miles and a good three thousand feet of height away, and as she runs down through the waterlogged fastness of Glen Dee, thousands of small streams act as tributaries to swell the river in a very short time. As a result, the narrow confines of the Linn of Dee acts as a great stopper to the waters of the river, and the resulting aquatic chaos is well worth witnessing.

The Linn, or narrows, is caused by the presence of a band of hard resistant rock which the river has only been able to cut down through very slowly and along a very constricted course. The Linn is set amidst a clutch of ancient Caledonian pines, and a picnic there is more often than not accompanied by a flock of semi-tame chaffinches, or, if you're really lucky, a crossbill or two.

A number of attractive walks are set around the uppermost part of the River Dee which is quite easily accessible by public road.

From Braemar drive along the winding minor road which heads west, gradually rising through twisted birch trees up the slopes on the south side of the valley, thus avoiding the broad and often waterlogged alluvial plains below. As the road levels out you get superb views up the length of the glen with the great domes and peaks of the high tops of the

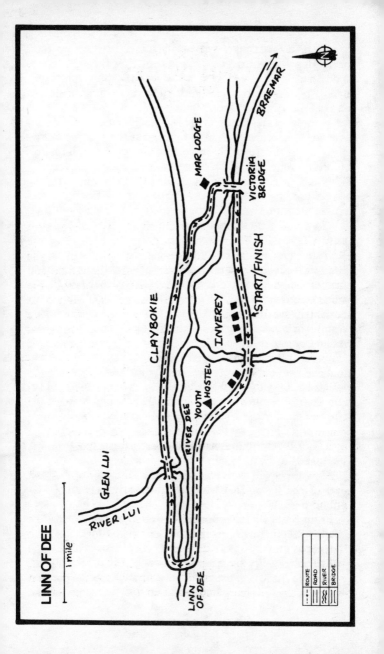

LINN OF DEE

1 mile

GLEN LUI

RIVER LUI

LINN OF DEE

RIVER DEE

YOUTH HOSTEL

CLAYBOKIE

MAR LODGE

INVEREY

START/FINISH

VICTORIA BRIDGE

BRAEMAR

| ROUTE |
| ROAD |
| RIVER |
| BRIDGE |

Cairngorms appearing tantalisingly close. Further on the road drops again to river level and continues through birch woods and conifer plantations towards the tiny village of Inverey. Park the car here and enjoy the couple of miles towards the Linn of Dee on foot.

A pleasant walk can be made by making a circuit of both banks of the Dee with the road bridge at the Linn and the footbridge at Inverey as the upper and lower limits. The main interest en route lies in the river and the ancient pine forest, with their associated wildlife. Crested tits can be seen here, as well as the crossbills, or Scottish parrots as they're often known. In winter the red deer herds come down from the high tops and seek their food within the shelter of the old forests.

On the river you're likely to see the dipper, that dapper little fellow of the riverside who'll often vanish below the tumultuous waters to feed on the river bed itself. And of course the River Dee is one of the finest salmon rivers in the highlands, and the Linn of Dee is an ideal place to spot them jumping and leaping upriver, one of the great natural phenomena of our country.

Inverey is the last place in Aberdeenshire where the Gaelic language held out as everyday speech. The old Celtic tongue was heard there up until the late 1920s. There's not a lot to Inverey – a telephone box, a Youth Hostel and a string of small houses, most of them let out nowadays as holiday cottages.

To start the walk, cross the old Ey bridge, just past the phone box, to Little Inverey, where a fine view of the western Cairngorms opens out. Ben MacDhui, the second highest mountain in Britain, can be seen, particularly its pointed crag which is situated above the Green Lochan, Lochan Uaine. Close by you'll see the fine cone of Derry Cairngorm while to the left lie the summit slopes of Braeriach above its Coire Bhrochain cliffs.

Enjoy the walk along the road, usually quiet and virtually unused, to the bridge over the Dee just above the Linn itself. A good view of the torrents can be had from the bridge. Other

The crashing waters of the River Dee, forced into a narrow chasm at the Linn of Dee.

parts of the Linn shouldn't be approached too closely except with proper footwear which won't slip on wet grass. Children should be watched carefully.

To return to Inverey take the road on the north bank of the river and follow it past the entrance to Glen Lui. The track up this glen forms one of the traditional routes into the high Cairngorms, a track once used by cattle drovers and now used by walkers, climbers and deerstalkers. You may notice some old sluices and concrete banks on the river close to this point. These are the remains of an old Canadian lumber camp which existed here during the 1939–45 war. To the north of here, hidden from the road, the River Lui crashes over some more superb waterfalls into fine green pools. This is a wonderful spot to sit if there are too many people around the Linn of Dee.

Continue on the road eastwards again, forking right on the road just past the houses at Claybokie. This will lead you past the imposing grandeur of the Mar Lodge Hotel, now sadly closed for much of the year but once the centre of a thriving deer stalking industry in Victorian times.

Cross the Victoria Bridge over the Dee again, and return to Inverey by walking westwards.

Walk 15
THE COLONEL'S BED
GRAMPIAN
7 miles

The Braemar area, or the Braes o'Mar as it is traditionally known, is one of great historical importance. One of the district's, and indeed Scotland's, greatest heroes was Malcolm III of Scotland, known throughout the highlands as Malcolm Ceann Mor, or Canmore, Malcolm of the Big Head, who died at the Battle of Alnwick in 1093.

Malcolm built the castle of Kindrochit, near Braemar, and bestowed the Earldom of Mar on the man who until then had been Captain of the district. Thus the Earldom of Mar stretches back almost a thousand years. Kindrochit castle, incidentally, was destroyed by artillery fire because its residents at the time were stricken with plague – the Galar Mor, or Great Plague.

Kindrochit Castle shouldn't be confused with Braemar Castle, which for a number of years now has been the private residence of the Farquharsons of Mar. The Farquharsons have been renowned in the district for some four centuries. It's claimed that they were descended from Farquhar, son of John Shaw of Rothiemurchus, who lived about 1370. A celebrated ancestor of the Farquharsons was Fionnlagh (Finla) Mor, or Big Finlay, a man of reputed great natural strength. Big Finlay was killed by a cannonball from an enemy ship at the Battle of Pinkie in 1547 when carrying the Royal Standard of Scotland. It was in the Farquharsons' house of Invercauld, just outside Braemar, that the Jacobite lords and chiefs, with the Earl of Mar as their leader,

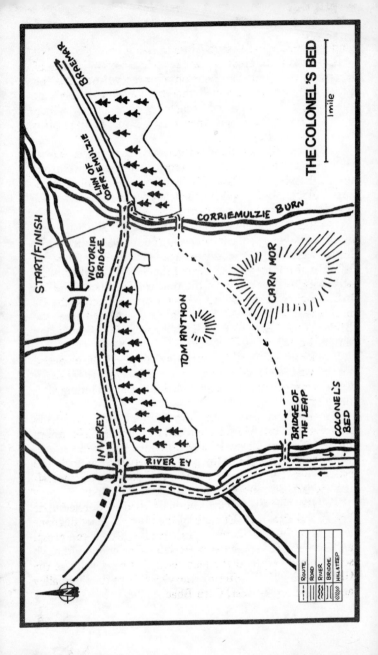

THE COLONEL'S BED

1 mile

BRAEMAR

START/FINISH

LINN OF CORRIEMULZIE

VICTORIA BRIDGE

CORRIEMULZIE BURN

CARN MOR

TOM ANTHON

INVEREY

RIVER EY

BRIDGE OF THE LEAP

COLONEL'S BED

N

		ROUTE
		ROAD
		RIVER
		BRIDGE
		HILL & STEEP

gathered before the first Jacobite uprising of 1715.

But perhaps the greatest legendary character in this area of legends is one John Farquharson of Inverey, known as the Black Colonel. It's claimed that he was in the habit of summoning his servants by firing his pistol at a shield which hung on the wall, which when hit by a bullet, gave off a bell-like tone.

One of the Black Colonel's legendary party-pieces was to ride his black mare up the steep rocky hill which rises from the north side of the Pass of Ballater. Seeing the huge crags and boulders on that hillside the feat appears incredible, yet there is little doubt Farquharson performed it.

The Black Colonel was something of a rebel and had many escapes from government troops. On one occasion they burnt his castle and he managed to escape not a moment too soon. With an almighty leap he cleared the River Ey, which was, according to the records of the time, in full flood. The old hump-backed bridge which takes the old road across the Ey near where he jumped is known as Drochaid an Leum, the Bridge of the Leap. The bridge is about a mile above where the road crosses the Ey today.

Farther up the River Ey is the Colonel's Bed, the objective for this walk – a ledge in a chasm of the river where the Black Colonel is reputed to have remained for a time in hiding after the burning of his castle.

Driving westwards along the Linn of Dee road from Braemar you can see on approaching Corriemulzie, about three miles from Braemar, a well-defined pass to the south-west of Corriemulzie. This pass lies between the little hill called Tom Anthon and Carn Mor and provides an interesting and pleasant short walk to the Colonel's Bed.

To start the walk, leave the main road at Corriemulzie bridge and take the east bank of the burn. A short distance along it you'll come across a little bridge, which you cross, and just beyond, some fine waterfalls. The going, although soft, is very easy and the glen itself, known locally as the Glack, is delightful, offering fine views down the Dee valley and, to the south-west, Carn Bhac.

The Colonel's Bed, an uncomfortable hiding place.

The descent can be made directly to Inverey through the pine woods, but your route proceeds westwards into lower Glen Ey. Cross the bridge over the Ey onto a Land Rover track on the opposite side and walk upstream for a mile or so to the Colonel's Bed. This is a ledge of rock in the side of a gorge through which the River Ey runs. The Ey, although appearing most of the time to be rather passive, cannot be crossed safely except at the bridges a mile below or half a mile above the Colonel's Bed.

The gorge itself is hardly noticeable from the moorland and although a well-defined track now leads to the spot the ledge can readily be conceived as having been an unusual but secure hiding place. This is the spot where Colonel John Farquharson found shelter and went into hiding after his castle had been burnt down shortly after the Battle of Killikrankie.

Take great care when making the descent to the actual ledge as the pools are very deep and would be very dangerous if you were to slip and fall in.

The return journey to Inverey is by the Land Rover track

which follows the Ey burn, and then by the main road back to Corriemulzie.

If you are only interested in viewing the Colonel's Bed, and don't have a lot of time, there is a shorter alternative to this walk. Walk up past the stalkers house on the south side of the road at Inverey and join the Land Rover track following the Ey burn all the way. The return journey is by the same route and you should allow yourself about two hours for the walk.

Walk 16
THE DUBH LOCH (BLACK LOCH)
OF LOCHNAGAR
GRAMPIAN

8 miles

Despite its name, Lochnagar isn't a loch but a mountain, and a fine one at that. It overlooks the royal country of Balmoral in Aberdeenshire and was a great favourite of Queen Victoria. The hill is possibly best known today as the title of one of Scotland's best loved songs, 'Dark Lochnagar', the words of which were written by Lord Byron. A children's book, 'The Old Man of Lochnagar', was written by no less an author than the Prince of Wales and published a few years ago. It apparently had its origins in a story that the Prince made up for his younger brothers while staying at Balmoral during the Royal summer holidays.

Close to Lochnagar and the village of Ballatar lies Loch Muick, and at its head, clenched in a deep-set mountain corrie, lies our objective – the Dubh Loch, a place of wild craggy hillsides and a superb wilderness atmosphere. This is the haunt of golden eagle and red deer – and climbers, in both summer and winter. The backcloth of dark brooding cliffs plunges down from the heights of Broad Cairn, and the setting well justifies the Gaelic name of Black Loch. This loch is much smaller than Loch Muick and being at an elevation of close on 2,000 feet can be covered with ice until well into the summer. Don't be tempted onto the ice, though, as it breaks up into great ice floes which can be difficult to get off.

If you're really lucky, you may spot a golden eagle or peregrine falcon up here, and from September to late Octo-

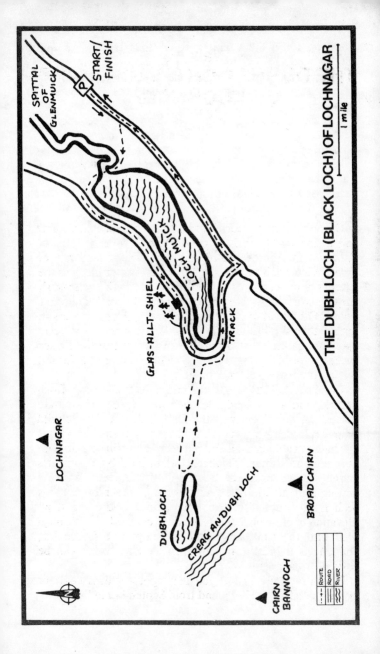

THE DUBH LOCH (BLACK LOCH) OF LOCHNAGAR

SPITTAL OF GLENMUICK

START/FINISH

P

LOCH MUICK

GLAS-ALLT-SHIEL

TRACK

DUBHLOCH

CREAG AN DUBH LOCH

LOCHNAGAR

CAIRN BANNOCH

BROAD CAIRN

N

1 mile

ROUTE
ROAD
RIVER

ber you'll hear the roaring of the rutting stags: a fine sound well suited to the mood of the place.

A good path circuits Loch Muick and it offers an attractive and easy low-level walk. At the head of Loch Muick another track branches off to climb up to the Dubh Loch. Loch Muick is a sizeable loch and lies about 1,300 feet above sea level. It's accessible by road from Ballater and offers a good starting point for many different excursions into these hills of Balmoral estate. There is a car park at the start of the walk and the surrounding area is a wildlife reserve, so don't be surprised to see herds of red deer grazing close to the road.

To reach the car park, cross the River Dee in Ballater (which lies about 40 miles east of Aberdeen, on the A93) and after about half a mile west on the south Deeside road turn left up the minor road which is signposted 'Glen Muick'. For the first five miles or so the road climbs gradually to the level of the upper valley floor, offering tantalising glimpses of the Falls of Muick on your right. After a short time, the tree-clad slopes change to a bare and featureless moorland, a treeless expanse which offers fine habitat for grouse, hare and deer. The road ends at a car park about a mile short of the loch and close by is an information hut.

Other walks from Glen Muick include Lochnagar itself (3,789 feet) and the Capel Mounth walk over into nearby Glen Doll and Glen Clova. Good Land Rover tracks circuit the whole perimeter of Loch Muick; once the deer are shot on the hill they are usually carried or dragged down to the track side where Land Rovers will come and pick them up.

From the car park walk past the interpretive centre and take the road which immediately strikes off across the valley floor, or alternatively keep straight on until just short of the near end of the loch where a track leads off to follow the shore. A good bridge crosses the river at this point.

From the shores of Loch Muick you can begin to realise the superb position of the place. On either side it is hemmed in by steep slopes of scree and heather, leading down over an abrupt edge from a virtual plateau which stops around the 2,000 feet mark. The loch is over 250 feet deep which

The Dubh Loch of Lochnagar, a remote and wild stretch of water amid the Royal land of Balmoral.

indicates perhaps that the valley was created by glaciation. As further proof of this theory the north end of the loch is dammed by glacial deposits now covered by deep peat.

Along either side of the loch are a few old birch trees, one of the species which used to flourish in these parts. Regeneration of the birch is now virtually impossible, simply due to the presence of red deer. Whenever the young shoots begin to show above the ground they're nibbled by hungry deer, so there is no chance of new growth.

On the north-west side of the loch, close to its southern end, stand the buildings of Glass Allt Shiel, a modest shooting lodge built on the instructions of Queen Victoria. The name of the lodge is taken from the tumbling burn which roars down from Lochnagar behind. If you have time, it's worthwhile taking a walk up by the burn to view the Glas Allt Falls, where the burn begins its plunge down from the plateau.

At the southern extremity of the loch one of the burns entering is the Allt an Dubh Loch, and on the north side of this stream an easy track leads upwards to the secluded Dubh Loch itself.

Return by the track to Loch Muick, but bear right, round the western end, so you can walk back to the car park by the shore opposite the one you followed earlier.

Walk 17
BENNACHIE IRON AGE FORT
GRAMPIAN
6 or 3 miles

Although little over 500 metres in height, Bennachie ranks as one of the best-loved landmarks in Aberdeenshire, and one of the best-known 'wee hills' in Scotland. Dominating the farm plains of the area known as the Garioch (pronounced Geeree), and the further low farmlands of Buchan, Bennachie is also a welcome landmark for fishermen returning to Aberdeen and the Aberdeenshire fishing ports after extended fishing trips to the North Sea. And indeed, many people who have never seen the hill will be familiar with the Aberdeenshire song which runs:

Oh, gin I were where the Gadie rins,
Far Gadie rins, far Gadie rins,
Oh, gin I were far Gadie rins,
At the fit o'Bennachie.

Many will know the song as a pipe tune which was adopted as the regimental march of the Gordon Highlanders. The Gadie, by the way, is the stream on the north side of the hill.

Gazing at Bennachie from a distance, on the long ridge of the hill its prominent tors at either end resemble breasts, and some believe that the name of the hill is taken from this feature, as in Beinn Chioch, or the hill of paps.

Bennachie, then, is a distinctive ridge, about three miles long, with a series of distinctive tops. The highest of the tops is the Oxen Craig (1,733ft) but the most interesting, and the best-known is the slightly shorter easternmost point called

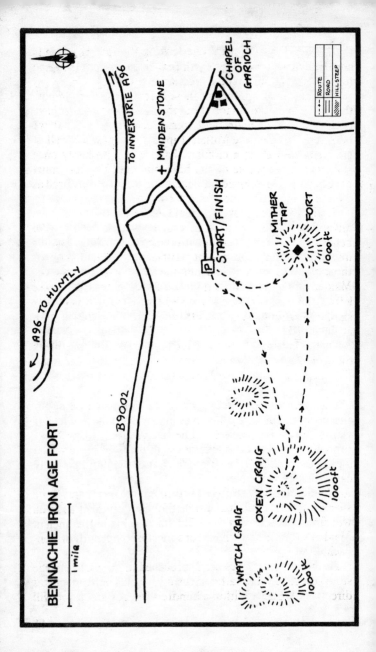

BENNACHIE IRON AGE FORT

1 mile

A96 TO HUNTLY

TO INVERURIE A96

B9002

MAIDEN STONE

CHAPEL OF GARIOCH

START/FINISH

P

MITHER TAP FORT 1000ft

OXEN CRAIG 1000ft

WATCH CRAIG 1000ft

·-·-	ROUTE
‖‖	ROAD
░░	HILL STEEP

the Mither Tap. Up here, overlooking the rich farm lands and the blue waters of the North Sea, lies an ancient Iron Age fortress sitting on top of a great granite block.

We know very little about these Pictish people, or of how they built these hilltop forts, but the construction must have taken many man-hours and tremendous effort. What we have remaining on the Mither Tap is a 15 foot thick wall of large stones built in a circular shape which probably once surrounded the whole of the hill's summit. The fort must have been of some considerable size and was probably used as a place of refuge by the Picts of the surrounding areas.

From Aberdeen, take the main A96 road to about three miles beyond the town of Inverurie. Just before the A96 bends right, at the junction with the B9002, turn left onto a minor road which leads to Chapel of Garioch. But after about three-quarters of a mile from the A96, just beyond the Maiden Stone – an inscribed Pictish standing stone just to the left of the road – take the road to the left which is clearly signposted 'Bennachie Car Park' and follow it to the car park at the end.

There is a choice of walks from here to the fort: the direct route to Mither Tap, no more than three miles in total, or the six mile route which takes the walker via Oxen Craig. The shorter is described first.

The ascent from the car park to the Mither Tap is about one and a half miles and involves just over a thousand feet of ascent, none of it too steep. The track is good all the way, although it crosses over several estate roads en route to the top. These are all marked 'private' so they shouldn't pose any navigational problems.

The first part of the ascent is through the forest and is the steepest. After about half a mile though it eases off and you will find yourself on a very old track. This is the ancient Maiden's Causeway, which runs most of the length of Bennachie.

As the summit slopes are approached the track leaves the stony causeway and after crossing a small stream makes directly to the top. Within a hundred feet of the top you will

Bennachie, a well-known landmark in Aberdeenshire and site of an ancient fort.

pass through the entrance of the fort where you will see how the stones have been built up to create this very thick wall. The path picks its way up stones to the top, and there are many fine variants to choose, particularly if you fancy the idea of a simple rock scramble.

The view from the summit is quite extensive, overlooking Aberdeenshire, Garioch, Feughside, Deeside and even as far as the Cairngorms. An indicator, implemented by Mr James McKey, Depute Senior Baillie of Bennachie was erected a few years ago with the help of teachers and pupils from Inverurie Academy.

In 1973 a local group called the Baillies of Bennachie was formed to look after the hills in view of the greatly increased number of visitors in recent years.

The longer route to the hill fort follows a path, completed in 1973 by the Forestry Commission, leading south from the car park then west through the woods to the top of Oxen Craig. From there, take the path eastwards to Mither Tap – another route established by the Forestry Commission, and a welcome one, for this long whaleback ridge of Bennachie is covered all year in deep heather, arduous to walk through. The descent from Mither Tap follows the route taken by the shorter walk.

Walk 18
BRUAR FALLS
TAYSIDE
$2\frac{1}{2}$ miles

I've often wondered just how many people race up and down the A9 Perth to Inverness road without knowing of the marvellous walk to the Bruar Falls, just a couple of miles north of Blair Atholl. I used to see the signpost every time I drove up and down the road before the Blair Atholl bypass was built, and I always made a promise to myself that one day I would stop and take a look. I did eventually, and was glad. I not only thoroughly enjoyed the walk, but realised that even in what appears to be fairly dense conifer plantation, often there are little scenic gems to be found.

That first visit to Bruar will stay in my mind for a long time, for all the way north the sun had been shining from a deep blue sky and a slight covering of early winter snow on the ground looked crystalline and delicate. The trees, particularly further south, were still in their full autumnal glory, and the higher hills just shone in the sunshine. Ahead of me I saw that the dark pass of Drumochter was frowning. There was a very black band of cloud forming a great barrier across the pass, so I was tempted into spending a couple of extra hours in the sun. Bruar proved ideal.

Robert Burns, Scotland's national bard, went to Bruar Falls in September 1787 when he was enjoying one of his Highland tours. Burns was a ploughman, a small farm tenant whose fame as a poet went before him. He was adopted by the literati of the time in Edinburgh who seemed quite taken by this rustic bard. Burns was, by all accounts, able to handle

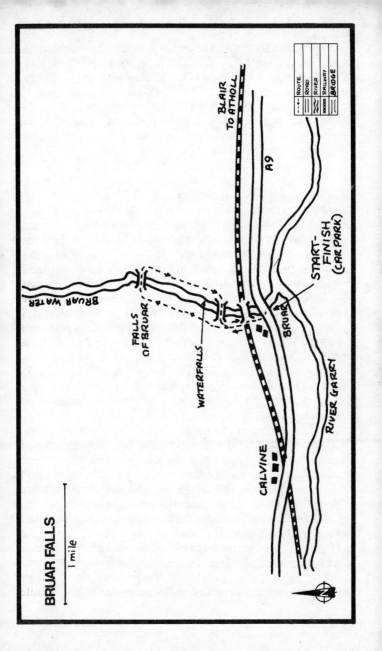

BRUAR FALLS

1 mile

BRUAR WATER

FALLS OF BRUAR

WATERFALLS

BLAIR TO ATHOLL

A9

START-FINISH (CAR PARK)

BRUAR

CALVINE

RIVER GARRY

| ROUTE |
| ROAD |
| RIVER |
| RAILWAY |
| BRIDGE |

himself very ably even with the nobility, thanks to his father who insisted, even at great expense, that Burns should receive an education. It certainly paid off for Burns, and his works are remarkable in their understanding of socialism at a time when such statements were almost unacceptable.

Anyway, despite his natural socialism, Burns mixed with lairds and nobles of the day, and indeed, on his visit to Atholl stayed with none other than the Duke of Atholl. While he was living here he was taken to Bruar Falls to be shown the attractions. Burns was obviously impressed by the rock features and the rushing waters, but he wasn't so struck by the bare moorlands which surrounded the streams. After his visit he wrote a short poem to the Duke of Atholl:

Wad then my noble master please,
To grant my highest wishes,
He'd shade the bank wi' towering trees,
And bonnie spreading bushes.

The verse had the desired effect and the poor ploughman poet, armed only with the simplicity of verse, motivated the rich and powerful Duke of Atholl into planting a vast wood around the falls, the woods which we can so enjoy today. A vote of thanks to Robert Burns.

Bruar itself is signposted on the new A9 road and there is a large car park beside the hotel. A signpost pointing through the trees shows the direction of the footpath which leads to the falls.

In a very short distance the magnificence of the falls becomes apparent. The water runs down through a fine chasm, steep sided and water worn. At one point the water rushes through the chasm below an ancient rustic bridge, and then drops again to flow through a natural archway of rock. If you stand on top of the bridges more falls enter the scene from above, again through a narrow natural chasm, to rush into a great pool of clear green water.

These are the real attractions of Bruar, and it's sad that so many people turn back at this point and retrace their steps back to the car park. In fact the path continues for another mile or so, up the length of the narrow glen through the

Bruar Falls, magnificent cascades amid superb woodland.

birches and rhododendrons bushes. The scenery isn't so dramatic here, with trees dominating everything, but at the head of the glen another bridge takes you over the stream and the path continues down the left bank dropping at one point close to the edge of a very steep drop.

From here the scene back up towards the top bridge is quite superb, reminiscent of one of those Chinese garden paintings. Conifers and birch swathe the slopes on each side of the cleft and the little hump-backed bridge appears to hold both sides of the glen together. Below it falls a long white slash of waterfall, and a bit below that more falls appear through the shrubbery. With a deep blue sky above and a lowering sun catching the golds, russets and browns of the birches, the scene can be quite exquisite. From here the path drops back down to the first bridge, and then back to the car park on the old A9.